STAR WARS™

BE MORE OBI-WAN

Written by Kelly Knox

Contents

The sage's path to staying grounded

The galaxy can be a stressful place. A big test coming up, difficulties at work, an interplanetary war against a droid army ... it can be overwhelming for even the most legendary guardians of peace and justice. And that doesn't even include clashing with your misguided best friend who recently turned to the dark side. But did you know you can overcome just about any obstacle by being true to yourself, and doing it with a smile?

Be More Obi-Wan guides you in using both your wisdom and your wit to handle whatever the galaxy throws at you. You'll learn to say "Hello there!" to your problems with grace, courage, and a well-timed joke or two—by learning from a Jedi Master.

FACING
CHALLENGES

When your troubles begin to pile up,
starting over as a reclusive old wizard
might sound pretty good. But life has a way
of bringing you back to the galaxy-size
problems you tried to leave behind.
Confront your challenges with grace—
and a plan—and you'll be unstoppable.

"Hello there!"
Obi-Wan Kenobi

Jump in feet first

The wisest Jedi Masters know that a moment will come when you need to greet your challenges head on. You've finished your meticulous planning and kept a cautious distance, and now it's time to jump right in and get to work. Toss off anything that might get in your way—like bulky Jedi robes or empty excuses—then roll up your sleeves and welcome your problems. And if you can throw in some impressive lightsaber moves as well? Even better. The obstacles before you don't stand a chance.

"I like firsts. Good or bad,
they're always memorable."
Ahsoka Tano

Consider failure just as valuable as success

As Ahsoka Tano learned from Obi-Wan Kenobi and Anakin Skywalker time and time again, no one is perfect. Even a Jedi can make a mistake! Getting started is often the hardest part of the process, whether it's struggling to levitate rocks with the Force or reaching a new goal in your career. Think of failure as simply the first step to success. And sometimes the second. And the third. What's important is continuing to move forward, on and on, until you find yourself where you want to be.

"We meet again, at last."
Darth Vader

Stop avoiding your problems

When it feels like the galaxy around you is almost unrecognizable, living alone in the desert for 20 years might sound very tempting. But unless you're actually being hunted by a powerful former-friend-turned-Sith, it's never a good strategy to avoid your challenges for too long. (Especially in the desert. Sand is irritating and gets everywhere.) Obi-Wan had to hide, but he also chose to tackle his problems by devoting himself to a new mission. Consider taking a different direction to refocus your efforts when overcoming obstacles.

"You have done that yourself!"
Obi-Wan Kenobi

Own up to your actions

It's easy to blame someone else when things start to blow up like an unstable lava planet. Take a hard look at yourself before pointing your lightsaber at others. Were you lashing out in anger, like Anakin? Take a moment to think about the situation you've found yourself in and how you may have caused it. Then fix the problems you've created. Sure, it could take years, and you might need some help from Luke Skywalker, but it's not too late to make things right.

"Confronting fear is
the destiny of a Jedi."
Luke Skywalker

Face your fears

Of course, even the most powerful Jedi can feel scared. From Rey to Anakin Skywalker, facing what they feared most was part of their journey to finding their true selves. You can choose to let fear consume you, as it does Obi-Wan's apprentice, or you can draw strength from acknowledging and accepting your fear. Then decide how to confront it. You can take steps as small as Grogu's little shuffle or leap in like Obi-Wan. No matter the path you pick, remember that you're as brave as a Jedi while you're on it.

KEEPING PERSPECTIVE

Have you ever been certain that someone was the Chosen One—only to find out they're not who you thought they were? Sometimes you have to look again or deliberately change your perspective to see what's really going on. You might be surprised to find what's true, from a certain point of view.

"Don't tell me what things look like.
Tell me what they are."
Leia Organa

See past the surface

Sometimes the truths we tell others—and ourselves—aren't the whole story. Are you expecting the worst or focusing on what might go wrong? Your worries might be distorting the reality of the situation. Maybe the entire galaxy isn't out to get you, for example. (Unless you're Han Solo.) Stick to the facts and look at what's really going on beneath the surface. Then reapproach the situation without excuses or exaggeration. Be honest with yourself and others—and you, too, can be unflappable, like General Leia Organa.

"Only a Sith deals in absolutes."
Obi-Wan Kenobi

Don't view everything in extremes

The galaxy isn't just black or white. There's so much to discover and explore in between! Declaring others as simply with you or against you proves your narrow mindset; you only want to do things your way or the hyperspace way. This deliberate unwillingness often leads to anger. Anger leads to hate, and ... well, you know the rest. Only Sith see the galaxy in such extremes. Do what you must to keep an open mind and even Master Yoda will call you wise.

"You have everything you need."
Luke Skywalker

Appreciate what you have

Okay, yes, maybe your recent efforts have literally crashed and burned. You might even feel like you're all alone on a remote island in the middle of a churning ocean. But there's always something in your life you can choose to be grateful for. Consider what you do have in this very moment, both visible and invisible—like support from the people on your side, hope, and a good backup plan—and appreciate it all.

"Don't let your personal feelings get in the way!"
Obi-Wan Kenobi

Remember the big picture

Legendary Jedi always put the greater good before
their own desires. That means there will be times
when you have to make some tough choices.
For instance, if you see your childhood crush in
danger, you might want to abandon your mission and
go straight to their rescue. But come to your senses!
They'd want you to finish the job and help turn the
tide of battle. Not to mention they can fend for
themselves with some quick thinking and
their tireless tenacity.

"So what I told you was true ...
from a certain point of view."
Obi-Wan Kenobi

Consider other points of view

Life is filled with hard truths. But how you choose to approach them can make a big impact. Maybe a loved one isn't ready to hear that their reckless father didn't listen to a thing you taught him and turned evil. However, you don't have to lie to them or yourself when tough questions are posed. Instead, look at the situation from a different angle, like Obi-Wan does when Luke asks about his father. It might lead to solutions more powerful than you could possibly imagine.

STAYING FOCUSED

Breathe. Just breathe. Renewing your focus begins with pausing to take in everything happening around you. Be mindful of the living Force—or just the present moment. Then you'll be ready to take your next step into the larger world. Just lift the blast shield on your helmet first.

"How did you know they wouldn't just attack us?"

"Because I make observations while you think with your lightsaber."

Anakin Skywalker and Obi-Wan Kenobi

Look before you leap

In a tight spot? Slow down and ponder the status quo before you make your next move. It might be tempting to rush in with lightsabers blazing—and that might even work occasionally, as Anakin Skywalker can attest. But to keep your cool like a Jedi Master, sometimes you'll need to pause and assess the circumstances before jumping into action. Use your eyes and ears instead of your laser sword, and you might be surprised to find out that not everything is as it seems.

"Keep your concentration here and now, where it belongs."
Qui-Gon Jinn

Focus on the present moment

Everyone can practice mindfulness, whether they're a Jedi Master like Qui-Gon Jinn or someone without a trace of any Force abilities. Mindfulness is the calming exercise of concentrating on what's happening in the present moment. Pay attention to the sights, sounds, smells, thoughts, and emotions surrounding you. Accept them all, even that unmistakable whiff of bantha poodoo. It's all too easy to let your mind wander into worries. But don't center on your anxieties! Focusing on the moment redirects your attention to *right now* instead of *what if.*

"Patience. Use the Force. Think."
Obi-Wan Kenobi

Take a breath

When a problem feels as big as a Hutt, sensible
Jedi know how to start working on a solution.
The first step you can take when you feel completely
overwhelmed is probably the most difficult:
be patient. Don't just rush off to solve everything like
you're running headlong after an assassin through
the back alleys of Coruscant! Re-center yourself with
a deep breath before you try to figure out what comes
next. *Then* it's time to act. Otherwise, you might drop
the ball (and your lightsaber) in your haste to find
a quick and easy solution.

"Stretch out with your feelings."
Obi-Wan Kenobi

Concentrate on your emotions

Everyday stresses or Force training wearing you down? Tune out the world (or starship) around you and turn your focus inward. What feelings bubble up to the surface? Imagine negative emotions like frustration stretching away from you until they disappear into nothing. Then send out your affection to those most important to you. Feel the support reaching back to you from friends and family no matter how far, far away they are. There's no mystical field controlling your destiny—*you* decide the energy you put out into the galaxy.

"Mind what you have learned.
Save you it can."
Yoda

Trust in your own experience

This is it. Everything you've learned through practice and real-world experience has prepared you for the test you're facing right now. Maybe it's clashing lightsabers with one of the galaxy's most fearsome foes. Perhaps it's a big project at work, or your final exams. Do you feel like a thousand terrible things are headed your way if you fail? Remember that you've trained hard to get to where you are. Trust in yourself and what your teachers have taught you. As Yoda says, "Already know you that which you need."

USING YOUR WIT(S)

You can handle what the galaxy throws at you with class *and* sass. A quick quip at the right time can relieve tension in a high-stress situation and disarm your enemies. Unless they have four arms. Then you might need to get ready for a fight.

"Then we decided to come
and rescue you."
"Good job."
Anakin Skywalker and Obi-Wan Kenobi

Allow yourself to smile in tough times

Sure, you're handcuffed in a dusty arena and surrounded by ferocious beasts, but that doesn't mean it's the wrong time to crack a joke. Nerve-wracking situations sometimes need a moment of levity so you don't feel like the jaws of an acklay are closing in around you. A wry one-liner delivered like the sass master Obi-Wan Kenobi can help break the tension. A quick smile might be what everyone needs as motivation to get going. *You'll* feel better, at the very least.

"So uncivilized."
Obi-Wan Kenobi

Use brute force as a last option

Like a true Jedi Master, you can strive to find an
elegant solution to whatever problem plagues you.
But when a plan falls apart and diplomacy fails,
sometimes there's only one option left. It's time
to abandon civility and fight for what you believe in!
Use everything at your disposal to pull off a victory.
Focus. Persistence. Improvisation. A wheel bike.
An electrostaff. It might feel like a clumsy and
random approach, but do whatever you can to get
to the heart of the matter when all else fails.

"Another happy landing."
Obi-Wan Kenobi

Keep your cool under pressure

Everything is falling apart, and the big boss is watching. Will you let yourself crash and burn? Of course not—you're smarter than that! Strap yourself into your starship and take the controls. Be the epitome of grace under pressure as you try to look on the bright side of a stressful situation. Then slow down, keep a level head, and do your best to ride it out. The result might not be a perfect landing, but you'll survive it if you just stay steady.

"These aren't the droids
you're looking for."
Obi-Wan Kenobi

Speak it into existence

Sometimes the first step in overcoming an obstacle or reaching your goals is to visualize exactly how you want it to happen. Then try saying it out loud, in order to trick the galaxy into making it real. (Or to just get rid of the two stormtroopers standing in your way.) The more you repeat your ambition out loud, the more you'll start to believe it yourself, and you'll work even harder to reach it. Now move along, move along, and start making your dreams come true.

"Lost a planet, Master Obi-Wan
has. How embarrassing,
how embarrassing!"
Yoda

Make a joke to make your point

A little good-natured banter can make a big impression when the timing is right. Yoda and Obi-Wan are masters—at using affectionate teasing to drive a point home. For Jedi Knights and anyone else who feels the weight of the galaxy on their shoulders, a joke can also be a much-needed reminder to not take themselves too seriously all the time. Make jokes to gently jest, never to anger, as that leads to the dark side. Be witty and wise, and your sense of humor will be long remembered.

BEING TRUE TO YOURSELF

Jedi Masters often take the time to reflect on who they are. What does your heart tell you? You must do what you feel is right and stay firm in your beliefs. You will always be challenged, but trust in the Force—and yourself—and you will persevere.

"Don't give in to hate. That leads to the dark side."
Obi-Wan Kenobi

Rise above negative feelings

Did you know Jedi Knights feel fear, anger, and hate just like everyone else? But they try to choose the light side of the Force instead and refuse to let negative emotions drive them or consume them. War, unimaginable loss, a sinister doctor picking a fight in the Mos Eisley Cantina: the galaxy is a lot to deal with. It's easy to get lost dwelling on all the things that give you a bad feeling. Don't give in! To Obi-Wan, you listen. You can choose the light side, too.

"Who's the more foolish, the fool,
or the fool who follows him?"
Obi-Wan Kenobi

Think for yourself

Who do you let guide you? Maybe it's the successful CEO of your company, or a Jedi Knight on some idealistic crusade. Take the time to reflect on who you're devoted to and where they might be leading you. The people you choose to follow says more about you than it does them. You'll know the good from the bad when you're calm and at peace. Here's a helpful tip: your new mentor declaring themselves the leader for life of a new Galactic Empire is a huge red flag.

"I'm sure another solution
will present itself."
Qui-Gon Jinn

Regroup and reassess when you need to

You've tried every solution to your problem that you can think of and nothing's working. Don't throw in the poncho! You might not see the answer right now, but be patient. Trust in the galaxy to provide you with more opportunities. Cool off, count midi-chlorians, eat dinner with new friends while you take shelter from a blinding sandstorm—whatever it is that helps you relax. Then take another look at your options. You'll see the problem with fresh eyes and a full stomach. Either way, you win.

"You can kill me, but you will never destroy me."
Obi-Wan Kenobi

Refuse to let anyone else define you

A Jedi has no shortage of enemies. Battle droids.
Bounty hunters. Sith. Really big fish. They may taunt
or tempt you, but they can't change you without your
permission. Only you have the power to define who
you are. If you give up what you believe in, then
they've already won the fight before you even ignite
your lightsaber. Keep believing. Yes, they may strike
you down, but it will be on your own terms, not theirs.

"I hate you!"
"You were my brother, Anakin.
I loved you."
Darth Vader and Obi-Wan Kenobi

Don't stoop to their level

Did a heated argument lead to a falling out with a former friend? Their destiny might lie on a different path than yours. Responding to hatred with more hatred is a hyperspace lane straight to the dark side. Rather than despise your enemies, turn your focus inward. Were you the one who failed them? What can you do to make it right? Obi-Wan responds to hate with love. Make the same choice, and the Force will be with you. Always.

Senior Editor Ruth Amos
Project Art Editor Jon Hall
Cover Artwork Dan Crisp
Production Editor Marc Staples
Senior Production Controller Mary Slater
Managing Editor Emma Grange
Managing Art Editor Vicky Short
Publishing Director Mark Searle

DK would like to thank: Brett Rector, Michael Siglain, and Troy Alders at Lucasfilm Publishing;
Kelsey Sharpe, Emily Shkoukani, and Kate Izquierdo at Lucasfilm Story Group;
Chelsea Alon at Disney Publishing; and Megan Douglass for proofreading.

First American Edition, 2022
Published in the United States by DK Publishing
1450 Broadway, Suite 801, New York, NY 10018

Page design copyright © 2022 Dorling Kindersley Limited
DK, a Division of Penguin Random House LLC
22 23 24 25 26   10 9 8 7 6 5 4 3 2 1
001-327542-July/2022

A catalog record for this book is available from the Library of Congress.
ISBN: 978-0-7440-5466-8

DK books are available at special discounts when purchased in bulk for sales promotions,
premiums, fund-raising, or educational use. For details, contact: DK Publishing Special Markets,
1450 Broadway, Suite 801, New York, NY 10018.
SpecialSales@dk.com

Printed and bound in China

For the curious

ww.dk.com
www.starwars.com

MIX
Paper from
responsible sources
FSC™ C018179

This book was made with Forest
Stewardship Council ™ certified
paper—one small step in DK's
commitment to a sustainable
future. For more information go to
www.dk.com/our-green-pledge